THE KING OF HEARTS

The Simplicity of Living in the Spirit

Don Walton

ISBN 0-9673498-0-X
Library of Congress Catalog Card Number: 99-93385

Press Worthy

May this book be used by God to lead many out of blackness and bondage into the marvelous light and liberty of our Lord Jesus Christ!

CONTENTS

INTRODUCTION

What the Scripture calls *"the flesh"* is almost universally interpreted to mean our old sinful or Adamic nature. Our sinful nature may best be defined as our natural inclination to sin. Given a choice between right and wrong the unregenerate man's natural propensity is to do wrong. This inborn bent toward sin is widely believed to be retained by Christians after their conversion. Hence, we have the struggle of the Christian life. Our old sinful nature, *"the flesh,"* pushes us to sin; our new Christlike nature, *"the Spirit,"* points us toward righteousness. We are tossed between the two as they pull us in opposite directions.

If this is true, what the vast majority believe about *"the flesh,"* then Christ only makes a halfway difference in our lives. He does a halfway job. Although He gives us a new nature at conversion, He does nothing about our old one. This popular, but foolish belief is refuted in *2 Corinthians 5:17* where the Apostle Paul writes, *"If any man be in Christ, he is a new creature, old things are passed away, behold, all things have become new."*

Our old nature, or natural inclination to sin, passes away when we come to Christ. It is replaced with a new nature: a divine one. According to the Apostle Peter, you and I become *"partakers of the divine nature"* in order to *"escape the corruption that is in the world through lust, (2 Peter 1:4).* In other words, partaking of the *"divine nature"* enables us to escape the world's corrupt practices by rendering sin undesirable to us. Sin looses its luster and is no longer lusted after. Consequently,

propensity becomes the practice of righteous-
ger are we prone to do what is wrong, but to do
and pleasing to God.

... ., *pians 2:12-13* the Apostle Paul instructs us to
"*work out [our] own salvation with fear and trembling, for it is God
that worketh in [us] both to will and to do of His good pleasure.*"
Notice, God is at work in us so that we will want to do, as
well as end up doing, God's "*good pleasure,*" or what pleases
Him. The Psalmist said the same thing in a different way
when he wrote, "*Delight thyself also in the Lord; and he shall give
thee the desires of thine heart,*" (*Psalm 37:4*). Many have misinterpreted this verse to mean that God will give us whatever we
desire. What this verse really teaches, however, is that God
will give us the desires themselves. He will work in our hearts
so that we will desire to do what pleases Him.

How do we "*work out our own salvation with fear and trembling?*" Obviously, we don't work out our salvation by working for it. Christ has already done all the work that needs to
be done for us to be saved. All that remains for us to do is to
accept by faith what Christ has done for us. When we do we
are saved by Christ's work, not by any works of our own, see
Ephesians 2:8-9.

We cannot work for our salvation. Nevertheless, we are
to work "*out*" our salvation. We work out our salvation by
trusting God's working within us and living out our daily
lives according to the dictates of our hearts. By following our
hearts we will be trusting God who is at work within them.
This explains why the Apostle Paul says that our salvation
must be worked out "*with fear and trembling.*" Working out in
our lives the salvation that God is working in our hearts is

tantamount to living our lives in a way that pleases God. It is not a mere matter of pleasing ourselves or pursuing our own fancies. It is a matter of us daily conforming externally to what God is performing in us internally.

In spite of this clear teaching from Scripture, we're taught today that we must not follow our hearts, because our hearts cannot be trusted. After all, doesn't *Jeremiah 17:9* teach us that our heart is *"deceitful above all things, and desperately wicked: who can know it?"* Although Jeremiah is accurately depicting the heart of a sinner in this verse: one who has not come to Christ, he is not describing the heart of a saint: one in whose heart Christ dwells, see *Ephesians 3:17*. How could Christ possibly live in the deplorable living conditions described by Jeremiah in Jeremiah 17:9?

In *Ezekiel 11:19-20* and *36:26-27* God talks about the New Covenant and promises to give us an *"undivided heart,"* as well as a *"new spirit,"* so that He can *"cause"* us to *"walk"* in His *"statutes"* and to *"keep"* His *"ordinances"* and *"judgments."* He even promises to remove our *"stony heart"* and replace it with a *"heart of flesh,"* so that we will be His people and He will be our God. There you have it! The New Covenant does not promise us a heart torn between two natures, as is preached in today's church, but a heart transplant, performed for us by the Great Physician.

> The New Covenant does not promise us a heart torn between two natures, as is preached in today's church, but a heart transplant, performed for us by the Great Physician.

In *Colossians 2:6* the Apostle Paul teaches us that we are to live for Christ the same way we received Him. We received

Christ by faith. We believed that His atoning work on the cross was enough to save us from our sins. We therefore trusted Christ to do for us what we could never do for ourselves. Now that we are saved from our sins, as a result of trusting in the sufficiency of Christ's saving work on the cross, we must live our lives trusting in the sufficiency of Christ's sanctifying work in our hearts. To put it more succinctly: We must stop trying to make our lives what they ought to be and start trusting Christ to do it for us.

When it comes to trusting Christ, we must not think of Him as being way up in heaven. Thanks to the indwelling Holy Spirit, Christ is not only in heaven—seated at the right hand of the Father—but He is also in our hearts! This is why the Apostle Paul wrote, *"But the righteousness which is of faith speaketh on this wise, Say not in thine heart, Who shall ascend into heaven? (that is to bring Christ down from above:) But what saith it? The word is nigh thee, even. . .in thy heart: that is, the word of faith, which we preach."* (Romans 10:6, 8).

We don't need to ascend into heaven to bring Christ down to help us. Christ is already with us. He is, as the Psalmist said, *"A very present help in trouble,"* (Psalm 46:1). Christ is as near to us as our own hearts, since He lives within them in the person of the Holy Spirit. In light of this, all we need to do to live by faith in Christ is to live our lives following our hearts. Whenever we are following our hearts we are trusting in the sufficiency of Christ's sanctifying work within us. On the other hand, whenever we are afraid to follow our hearts we are doubting the indwelling Christ.

Contrary to popular opinion, a Christian can follow his heart, since God has given him a new one at conversion.

God gives the Christian a new heart so that Christ can take up residence within it. Christ cannot possibly move into our old sinful heart of stone. Therefore, God replaces it at conversion with a new heart so that Christ can have adequate living accommodations in our lives. Once Christ moves in, we can begin following our heart. When we do, we will be trusting Him who is living and working within it. By following our heart, or living by the dictates of the Spirit's still small voice within us, we will be living in the Spirit.

THE CREATION OF MAN

When God created man and breathed into his nostrils the breath of life, *"man became a living soul,"* (Genesis 2:7). Man is a soul. This is why the Bible says, *"He which converteth the sinner from the error of his way shall save a soul from death,"* (James 5:20). The soul is the real you. It is the seat of your personality. It is your mind, will and emotions.

When God created man as a living soul He housed him in a physical body. God did this for two reasons. First, God gave man a physical body so that man could manifest God's glory. God is invisible, (*Colossians 1:15; 1 Timothy 1:17, Hebrews 11:27*). Thus, God created man with a physical body so that man could visibly display God's glory. In *Romans 1:20* the Apostle Paul explains how God created the visible world so that He could display His invisible qualities. Man, being the crowning act of God's creation, displays and manifest the invisible qualities of God more than anything else God has created.

The second reason that God gave man a physical body was so that man could have contact and communion with the physical world. It is through your body, in particularly through your five senses, that you have contact with the physical world. Without your body your contact with the physical world would be severed, as is made unmistakably clear by physical death. When someone dies they lose all contact with the physical world, not because their soul ceases to exist, but because it is no longer clothed with a physical body. The physical body has perished and been put off by the soul.

When God created man He not only housed him in a physical body, but He also placed within him, within the soul, a spirit. The spirit and soul are so intertwined that the Scripture often speaks of them interchangeably. In fact, the

Bible teaches that only the *"quick and powerful"* Word of God, which *"is sharper than any twoedged sword,"* can pierce deep enough *"to divide asunder soul and spirit,"* (Hebrews 4:12).

The reason God put a spirit within man was so that man could have contact with the spiritual world and communion with Him. Just as man has contact and communion with the physical world through his body, he has contact with the spiritual world and communion with God through his spirit. This is why the Psalmist said, *"Deep calleth unto deep,"* (Psalm 42:7). God's Spirit calls out to man's spirit and the spirit deep within man calls out to God. It is spirit to spirit communication. As the Apostle Paul said, *"The Spirit itself beareth witness with our spirit, that we are the children of God,"* (Romans 8:16).

When God created man man's spirit, not his body, was dominant. Man lived in constant communion with God. He walked and talked with God in the garden in the cool of the day, *(Genesis 3:8)*. Walking and talking with God enabled man to live his life by the information he received from God through his spirit. Man lived, as he was created to, *"by every word that proceeded out of the mouth of God,"* *(Matthew 4:4)*.

God created man as a spiritual being with a physical body, not as a physical being with a spirit. This is part of what the Bible means when it teaches us that we were created in the image of God, *(Genesis 1:26)*. Like God, you and I are spiritual beings.

Not only did God make us in His image by creating us as spiritual beings, but also by creating us as triune beings. God is a trinity. There is God the Father, God the Son and God

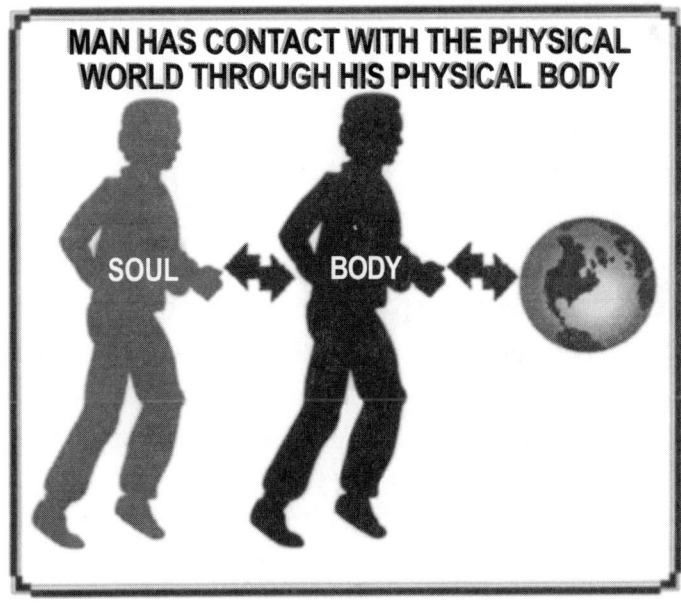

MAN HAS CONTACT WITH THE PHYSICAL WORLD THROUGH HIS PHYSICAL BODY

SOUL ← → BODY ← →

the Holy Spirit. All three are different, but all three are one. Likewise, man is a triune being, *(1 Thessalonians 5:23)*. We are soul, body and spirit. All three are different, but all three are one.

In *Genesis 1:26* God said, *"Let us make man in our image, after our likeness."* Notice, God did not say, *"I will make man in my image, after my likeness."* I believe the plural pronouns employed by God in this verse point to the Trinity. God made us triune like Himself. Our soul corresponds with God the Father. Our body corresponds with God the Son, who was *"made flesh and dwelt among us,"* *(John 1:14)*. And of course our spirit corresponds with God the Holy Spirit. No wonder King David exclaimed, *"I will praise thee; for I am fearfully and wonderfully made,"* *(Psalm 139:14)*.

THE FALL OF MAN

The darkest chapter in the Bible is the third chapter of Genesis. In this chapter we are told about the fall of man. When man sinned against God in the Garden of Eden the greatest tragedy of all time occurred. God withdrew His Spirit from man's spirit and man died spiritually. Spiritually dead, man no longer had contact with the spiritual world nor communion with God. He was separated and cut off from his Creator, because of sin.

In *Genesis 2:17* God warned Adam that *"in the day"* he ate of *"the tree of the knowledge of good and evil"* he would *"surely die."* Obviously, Adam did not die physically on the same day he sinned against God by eating of the tree of the knowledge of good and evil. In fact, the Bible teaches us that Adam went on to live 930 years of physical life, *(Genesis 5:5)*. Nevertheless, Adam did die the same day he sinned against God and fell in the garden. He died spiritually, not physically.

Spiritually dead, Adam no longer had contact with the spiritual world nor communion with God. He was reduced to living his life by the five senses of his physical body and the information they provided him from the physical world. Since Adam chose to eat of the tree of the knowledge of good and evil, he was left to process the information his five senses provided him from the physical world with nothing more than his own understanding.

As if this sorry state of affairs was not bad enough, it was made even worse by the fact that Adam's sin subjected his physical body, as well as the whole physical world, to corrup-

tion, see *Romans 8:19-23*. Nothing was as it should be nor as it was created to be anymore. Everything was fallen. Thus, man was left to live his life by the faulty information he received from a fallen world through the five senses of his fallen body, not to mention the fact, that he had nothing to figure it all out with except his own corrupt mind.

This deplorable state of spiritual death has been the plight of all men ever since the sin of Adam. However, we haven't suffered this fate merely because of Adam's sin, but also because of our own. As the Apostle Paul teaches us in *Romans 5:12*, "*Wherefore, as by one man sin entered into the world, and death by sin; and so death passed upon all men, for that all have sinned.*"

This sad state of living spiritually dead to God by the faulty information of a fallen world received through the five senses of a fallen body and processed by the understanding of a corrupt mind is what the Bible calls "*the flesh.*" It is from this sad state, caused by ours and Adam's sin, that Christ came to save us.

Although our dire need of Christ's salvation is made abundantly clear by the present consequences of our fallen condition, it becomes even more obvious when you and I consider the eternal outcome. According to the Bible, when one dies his body returns to dust, *(Genesis 3:19)*, his spirit to God who gave it, *(Ecclesiastes 12:7)*, and his soul goes to

> This sad state of living spiritually dead to God by the faulty information of a fallen world received through the five senses of a fallen body and processed by the understanding of a corrupt mind is what the Bible calls "*the flesh.*"

heaven or hell, (*Revelation* 6:9, *James* 5:20). If you go to heaven when you die your spirit returns to God intact with your soul to enjoy eternal communion with the Lord. If you go to hell, however, your spirit returns to God and your spiritless soul alone is confined to hell with no hope of ever communing with the Lord. This is the fearful eternal state of the spiritually dead, as well as the most solemn teaching in all of Scripture.

THE SALVATION OF MAN'S SOUL

The only way for man to be saved from his sin and reconciled to God is through faith in the Lord Jesus Christ. There is absolutely nothing you and I can do to save ourselves from spiritual death and to restore our communion with God. It is because of this hopeless and helpless lost condition of ours that Christ came into our world to do for us what we could never do for ourselves. Through His life, death and resurrection Christ has done everything necessary for our salvation. All that remains to be done is for us to accept by faith all that Christ has done for us.

In order for you and I to make ourselves righteous before God we must meet the requirements of God's Law. What God's Law requires is sinless perfection, see *Galatians 3:10* and *James 2:10*. Obviously, such a requirement is far beyond the reach of fallen sinners like you and I. Thus, as the Apostle Paul teaches, none of us have any hope of ever being right with God by living up to the Law, *(Romans 3:20, Galatians 2:16)*.

Since you and I cannot possibly live a sinless life in order to become righteous before God, Christ came and lived a sinless life for us. By living His sinless life in our place Christ fulfilled God's Law so that we don't have to, *(Matthew 5:17)*. All we have to do is accept by faith the righteous life that Christ lived for us. When we do, Christ's righteousness becomes ours and we become righteous before God because of the life Christ lived, not because of the life we're living. This is why the Apostle Paul calls Christ *"our righ-*

teousness," (1 Corinthians 1:30). It is also why he wrote that he wanted to *"be found in [Christ], not having [his] own righteousness, which is of the law, but that which is through the faith of Christ, the righteousness which is of God by faith,"* (Philippians 3:9).

> By living His sinless life in our place Christ fulfilled God's Law so that we don't have to, *(Matthew 5:17)*. All we have to do is accept by faith the righteous life that Christ lived for us. When we do, Christ's righteousness becomes ours and we become righteous before God because of the life Christ lived, not because of the life we're living.

In order to save us from our sins and reconcile us to God Christ had to do more than just live in our place. He also had to die in our place. Not only did He have to live a righteous life so that we could be righteous, but He also had to die for our sins so that we could be forgiven.

Before our sins against God can ever be forgiven our sin debt must be paid. God, being just, can never wink at our sins or just simply overlook them. He has to demand payment in full, lest He cease to be just. His justice demands that our sin debt be paid off before any pardon can be offered.

What is the debt of sin? According to the Bible, *"The wages of sin is death,"* (Romans 6:23). Wages are something you earn. Every sinner in this world is sentenced to death, because we've earned it. However, it is not just physical death that is our just deserts, but also spiritual death. Our rebellion against God has not only earned us an end to our temporal lives, but also the loss of eternal life. Our sins against God have earned us an eternal separation from Him.

For every sin that has ever been committed someone must surely die. Not one sin can go unpunished, but all must be paid for. This is why *Hebrews 9:22* says, "*And almost all things are by the law purged with blood; and without the shedding of blood is no remission.*" Since "*life is in the blood,*" see *Leviticus 17:11*, blood must be shed and life poured out before any sin can be forgiven. In other words, the only hope we have of being forgiven of our sins and escaping death is if someone should shed their blood in place of ours and dare to die in our place!

Since you and I cannot pay the sin debt we owe to God, Christ came into the world to pay it for us on the cross. By shedding His blood in place of ours and dying in our place Christ has made it possible for you and I to be forgiven of our sins and reconciled to God. All we need to do is accept by faith Christ's substitutionary death upon the cross for us. When we do, Christ gives us from His own nail scarred hand a receipt for our sin debt. This receipt written in Christ's own blood reads, "PAID IN FULL"! Just as the old hymn declares:

> "Jesus paid it all,
> All to Him I owe;
> Sin had left a crimson stain;
> He washed it white as snow."

That Jesus paid it all is proven by His triumphant shout from the cross, "*It is finished,*" (John 19:30). This Greek word "*telelestai*" literally means "*paid in full.*" Papyri receipts from the time of Christ have been recovered with the word "*telelestai*" written across them. Just before He "*bowed his head, and gave up the ghost*," Christ shouted "*paid in full*" across the sin debt of the world.

> Just before He "bowed his head, and gave up the ghost," Christ shouted "paid in full" across the sin debt of the world.

Even more important to our salvation than the substitutionary death He died or the righteous life He lived, is Christ's resurrection from the dead. In fact, the Apostle Paul says that the whole of our Christian faith hinges on this historical event. According to Paul, "*If Christ be not risen, then is our preaching vain, and our faith is also vain. Yea, and we are found false witnesses of God; because we have testified of God that he raised up Christ: whom he raised not up,*" (1 Corinthians 15:14-15). Paul goes on to add that without Christ's resurrection you and I are still "*in our sins,*" those who "*are fallen asleep in Christ are perished,*" and "*we are of all men most miserable,*" (1 Corinthians 15:17-19).

When Christ died on the cross He did more than just die for our sins, according to the Scripture He actually became our sin, (2 Corinthians 5:21). When Christ became our sin on the cross God the Father poured out the full fury of His wrath on Christ for every sin that has ever been committed, or that ever will be. On the cross Christ suffered the full punishment for every sin man has committed in the past, is committing in the present, or will commit in the future. This is why Christ, already kneeling under the shadow of the cross, suffered such agony in the Garden of Gethsemane, see *Matthew 26:36-45* and *Luke 22:39-46*.

It was not His shrinking back from the physical pain and

death of the cross that caused Christ's sweat to become like *"great drops of blood."* Instead, it was His becoming the sin of the world and suffering the full brunt of His Father's wrath. Although the physical death Christ died on the cross would be more than enough to make most men sweat blood, it was the spiritual death that He was facing that caused Christ's anguish in Gethsemane.

The fact that Christ experienced spiritual death, separation from God the Father, is made abundantly clear by Christ's blood curdling cry from the cross, *"My God, my God, why hast thou forsaken me,"* (Matthew 27:46). When Christ died on the cross, becoming the sin of the world, God the Father turned His back on His Son. He could no longer look upon His Son, now that His Son had become the sin of the world.

With God the Father turning His back and Christ—the Light of the world—becoming the sin of the world, is there any wonder that the earth was suddenly shrouded in an inexplicable darkness, *(Matthew 27:45)?* Suspended between heaven and earth, Christ was forsaken by both as He hung that dark day on the cruel cross of Calvary. Alone and abandoned Christ died for you and I.

Following His death, Christ's body was taken down from the cross and buried in a borrowed tomb. From the time of Christ's interment until He arose on that first Easter Sunday morning the drama of all the ages was played out. Could Christ, ensepulchered in the stead of all the sinners of the world, ever come alive to God again? This question for the ages, posed by Christ's occupied tomb, was resoundingly answered in the affirmative by His empty one.

Christ, who had become as spiritually dead to God as all the sins of the world could make Him, came back alive to God when He arose from the dead on that first Easter Sunday morning. This is why the Apostle Peter teaches that Christ was made alive in the spirit when He arose from the dead, *(1 Peter 3:18)*. Since Christ, who became the sin of the whole world, came back alive to God, so can the vilest of sinners who will *"believe in his heart that God has raised* [Christ] *from the dead,"* *(Romans 10:9)*. No matter how spiritually dead to God you are in your trespasses and sins, you too can come alive to God through faith in the resurrected Christ. This hope of spiritual life is the very heart of the Gospel and the reason it all hinges upon Christ's resurrection.

> Since Christ, who became the sin of the whole world, came back alive to God, so can the vilest of sinners who will *"believe in his heart that God has raised* [Christ] *from the dead,"* *(Romans 10:9)*.

In *Psalm 2:7* God the Father says to Christ *"Thou art my Son; this day have I begotten thee."* Being eternal and without beginning or end, when was Christ ever begotten by the Father? According to the Apostle Paul, Christ was begotten by the Father when He was raised from the dead. In *Acts 13:33* Paul says, *"God hath fulfilled the same unto us their children, in that he hath raised up Jesus again; as it is written in the second psalm, Thou art my Son, this day have I begotten thee."*

Did you know that Jesus Christ was the first person to ever be born again? He was the first to come back alive to God after being spiritually dead to Him, because of sin.

However, Christ's spiritual death was not a result of His sin, but of Him becoming ours. When Christ arose, coming back alive unto God, God the Father said to Him, *"Thou art my Son, this day have I begotten thee."*

As *"the first born from the dead,"* or the first to ever come back alive to God after being spiritually dead to Him, Christ has become *"the head of the body, the church,"* (*Colossians 1:18*). What is the church? It is simply all those, like Christ, who have been born again. The church is made up of those who were once dead to God in their trespasses and sins, but have now come alive to God through faith in the resurrected Christ.

According to the Apostle Paul, everyone in the church has been foreknown and predestined by God *"to be conformed to the image of his Son, that he might be the firstborn among many brethren,"* (*Romans 8:29*). God wants to have many more born again children to whom He can say, on the day they place their faith in His firstborn Son, *"Thou art my* [child], *this day have I begotten thee."* All of those begotten by the Father through faith in His risen Son become Christ's *"brethren"* and a part of Christ's body, the *"church of the firstborn,"* (*Hebrews 12:23*).

THE REBIRTH OF MAN'S SPIRIT

When we place our faith in the Lord Jesus Christ for salvation He comes to live within us in the person of the Holy Spirit. The Holy Spirit comes to indwell our spirit and we are born again, *(John 3:3)*. What part of us is born again? It is our spirit, not our soul nor our body, *(John 3:5-8)*. Although our appearance (body) and personality (soul) will be affected by the rebirth of our spirit, we do retain the same body and personality after being born again.

In *Ephesians 2:1* the Apostle Paul teaches us how we were dead in our *"trespasses and sins"* before we came to Christ. How were we dead before coming to Christ? We were spiritually dead. It was not our soul nor our body that was dead, but our spirit. Paul goes on in *Ephesians 2:4-5* to teach how coming to Christ results in us being *"quickened,"* or made alive. What part of us is made alive when we come to Christ? Again, it is our spirit, not our soul nor our body, which were both alive already.

Once we place our faith in the Lord Jesus Christ we can once again have contact with the spiritual world and communion with God through our reborn spirit. Our spirit can regain the ascendancy in our lives God always intended for it to have. We can live, as God created us to, in communion with Him and by every word that proceeds out of His mouth, *(Deuteronomy 8:3, Matthew 4:4)*. This is spiritual life and what the Bible calls living in the Spirit.

The reborn child of God is no longer to live in *"the flesh."* That is, he is no longer to live by the faulty information of a fallen world received through the five senses of his fallen body and processed by the understanding of his corrupt mind. Instead, he is to live in *"the Spirit."* He is to live by every word Christ speaks to his reborn spirit through the person of the Holy Spirit who dwells within him.

Adam, before the Fall, was spiritually alive in an incorruptible world, as well as clothed in an incorruptible body. Thus, Adam's unfallen world, senses and understanding were in perfect harmony with his spirit. Everything the unfallen world was communicating to Adam through the five senses of his unfallen body and the understanding of his unfallen mind was in perfect accord with everything God's Spirit was communicating to Adam's spirit.

You and I, as today's reborn children of God, are not like

ADAM BEFORE THE FALL

Adam before the Fall. We do not find ourselves spiritually alive in an incorruptible world. Neither do we find ourselves housed in incorruptible bodies. Instead, we find ourselves living in a corruptible world and imprisoned in corruptible bodies. Thus, our fallen world, senses and understanding are not in perfect harmony with our reborn spirit, but contrary to it. In fact, what the fallen world communicates to us through the five senses of our fallen bodies and the understanding of our corrupt minds is often a complete contradiction of what Christ is saying to our reborn spirits through the person of the Holy Spirit who lives within us. This is why the Apostle Paul wrote to the reborn children of God in Galatia, *"For the flesh lusteth against the Spirit, and the Spirit against the*

THE CHRISTIAN TODAY

flesh: and these are contrary the one to the other: so that ye cannot do the things ye would," (Galatians 5:17).

In *Romans 7:7-25* the Apostle Paul talks about the struggle in his spiritual life. According to him, his *"inward man,"* or reborn spirit, *"delighted in the law of God."* Paul's reborn spirit, just like yours and mine, wanted to do what God wanted him to. Paul's problem, however, was that his *"flesh"*—his fallen body with its fallen senses and understanding—was waging war against his spirit *"bringing [him] into captivity to the law of sin."* As a result of this struggle, Paul found himself not doing the *"good"* his reborn spirit desired to do, but the *"evil"* his flesh kept dragging him into. His fallen body's seeming upper hand over his reborn spirit was so grievous to the great Apostle that he cried out in *Romans 7:24, "O wretched man that I am! who shall deliver me from the body of this death?"*

In Paul's day the corpse of a murderer's victim was often strapped to the murderer's back. As the corpse decayed and rotted the murderer became diseased and died. This most cruel means of execution is what Paul was alluding to when he asked the question, *"Who shall deliver me from the body of this death?"* Paul saw his flesh, in particular his fallen body, as something he was strapped with in this fallen world. To him, the corruptible body to which he was tied in this corruptible world was not only subjecting him to disease and death, but was also most detrimental to his spiritual life. It was constantly hindering and hampering him from living in the Spirit. No wonder Paul concludes Romans Chapter 7 by thanking God that someday he would be delivered from *"the body of this death. . .through Jesus Christ our Lord,"* (Romans 7:25).

This struggle between flesh and spirit was mentioned by our Lord in *Matthew 26:41*. Here, Jesus realizes that His disciples were willing in their spirits to do what He wanted them to do; to watch and pray with Him. Their problem, however, was that their flesh was weak. Consequently, they kept being rocked to sleep by their fallen bodies, instead of spurred on to prayer by their willing spirits. Every reborn child of God is willing in their spirit to do what Christ wants them to do, but it is our flesh that is weak, or uncooperative.

> Every reborn child of God is willing in their spirit to do what Christ wants them to do, but it is our flesh that is weak, or uncooperative.

In *1 John 3:9-10* the Apostle John writes, *"Whosoever is born of God doth not commit sin; for his seed remaineth in him: and he cannot sin, because he is born of God. In this the children of God are manifest, and the children of the devil: whosoever doeth not righteousness is not of God, neither he that loveth not his brother."* Is John teaching us in these two verses that Christians do not sin? If so, he is contradicting what he has already taught us in chapter one of this epistle. In *1 John 1:8* John wrote, *"If we say that we have no sin, we deceive ourselves, and the truth is not in us."* In *1 John 1:10* he accents 1 John 1:8 with these additional words, *"If we say that we have not sinned, we make [God] a liar, and his word is not in us."*

Obviously, John is not contradicting himself. Neither is he teaching us that the sure sign of a saint is sinlessness. We all sin, Christians and non-Christians alike. We may even struggle with besetting sins, those which we continually trip over in our Christian walk, see *Hebrews 12:1*. Nevertheless, for a Christian to sin he has to go squarely against the grain of everything in him. This inward resistance to sin is the sure sign of one's salvation and the whole point John is trying to make in these two verses.

According to John, everyone who *"is born of God,"* or born again, has God's *"seed"* in him. Who is God's seed? God's seed is His Son Jesus Christ. Jesus Christ lives in every born again child of God. He

> For a Christian to sin he has to go squarely against the grain of everything in him.

lives in us in the person of the Holy Spirit. As a result, we *"cannot sin"* unless we fight our way through the resistance of the indwelling Holy Spirit. If we are successful in fighting our way through to sin, in spite of the Holy Spirit's constraining us from it, we will then find ourselves engaged in a whole new struggle. No longer will we be fighting against the Spirit so that we can sin, but now we'll be wrestling with a guilty conscience because we have sinned. Instead of the Holy Spirit constraining us from it, He will now be convicting us for it. In the face of all of this the reborn child of God will think twice before sinning again.

This inward struggle with the indwelling Holy Spirit faces every reborn child of God every time we sin. Therefore, John writes, *"Whosoever is born of God doth not commit sin."* Anyone continuing to live in sin cannot possibly be indwelt by the Holy Spirit. If they were, their inward struggle with God's Spirit would be too great for sin's continuance. Thus, the Apostle John is safe in saying that anyone who is not being constrained from sinning and compelled to do *"righteousness"* by God's indwelling Spirit *"is not of God."*

Did you know that the reborn children of God do not have to wait to receive the spiritual blessings of heaven? According to *Ephesians 1:3*, we already have *"all* [the] *spiritual blessings in heavenly places in Christ."* It is true that we do not presently possess all the physical blessings of heaven, such as a glorified body. Yet, we are already the recipients of all of heaven's spiritual blessings. We don't have to wait till we die to enjoy heaven's spiritual blessings. You and I can enjoy a little heaven right here on earth.

In *Colossians 2:9-10* the Apostle Paul explains how *"all the fullness of the Godhead"* dwells in Christ and how you and I *"are complete in him,"* because He dwells in us. If all of God is in Christ and Christ is in us then what could we possibly be lacking in ourselves? The clear and unmistakable answer is nothing. Since we have Christ we have it all. We are *"complete"* spiritually in Him. Our reborn spirits are fine. God's redemptive work in them is finished.

If we have all of God in us, as well as all the spiritual blessings of heaven right here and now, then why the struggle in our spiritual lives? Remember what the Apostle

Paul says in Romans Chapter 7. The struggle in our spiritual lives is caused by our *"flesh."* That is, our spiritual struggle is a result of the fact that you and I are imprisoned in fallen bodies and inhabitants of a fallen world. As Paul points out in *2 Corinthians 4:7, "We have this treasure in earthen vessels."* Although God's redemptive work is complete in our reborn spirits, our reborn spirits are still housed in fallen bodies. Hence, we have the struggle of the Christian life. Our unredeemed bodies are always wrestling with and warring against our redeemed spirits. The *"treasure"* on the inside is in conflict with and concealed by the *"earthen vessel"* on the outside.

> If all of God is in Christ and Christ is in us then what could we possibly be lacking in ourselves? The clear and unmistakable answer is nothing. Since we have Christ we have it all.

THE REDEMPTION OF
MAN'S BODY

In *2 Corinthians 5:1-9* the Apostle Paul refers to our fallen bodies as the *"earthly house of this tabernacle."* According to Paul, once our fallen bodies are *"dissolved"* we will receive a glorified body, or *"a building of God, an house not made with hands, eternal in the heavens."* Until then Paul says *"we groan, earnestly desiring to be clothed upon with our house which is from heaven."* Paul adds, however, that *"we that are in this tabernacle"* are not groaning to *"be unclothed, but clothed upon, that mortality might be swallowed up of life."* In other words, we are not necessarily groaning to escape from our fallen bodies through death, although Paul does express his preference for being *"absent from the body and. . .present with the Lord,"* but we are hoping to be alive when Christ comes. If we are, we will never die and be *"unclothed,"* or without a body. Instead, we will be *"clothed upon"* as our glorified body is put on over our fallen body so *"that mortality might be swallowed up of life."*

When someone dies their soul and spirit depart from their body and their fallen body is left behind as a corpse. The corpse returns to dust, just as God promised in *Genesis 3:19.* If the person who dies is not a born again child of God then their spirit returns to God who gave it, see *Ecclesiastes 12:7,* and their spiritless soul goes to hell with no hope of ever communing with God. On the other hand, if the person is a born again child of God their spirit returns to God intact with their soul to enjoy eternal communion with

Him. Nevertheless, having left their fallen body behind and having not yet received their glorified body, the born again child of God will remain *"unclothed"* in God's presence, or without a body, until they return with Christ and the resurrection occurs.

In *1 Thessalonians 4:13-14* the Apostle Paul writes, *"But I would not have you to be ignorant, brethren, concerning them which are asleep, that ye sorrow not, even as others which have no hope. For if we believe that Jesus died and rose again, even so them also which sleep in Jesus will God bring with him."* Every born again child of God who dies before Christ returns will return with Christ when He comes. How will they return with Christ? Since their fallen bodies were put off at death and their glorified bodies have not yet been resurrected they will have to return with Christ in a bodiless state. When they do; their graves will be opened, their glorified bodies resurrected and their resurrected bodies will rise to be united with their spirits and souls in the air, see *1 Thessalonians 4:15-18*. Afterward, they shall *"ever be with the Lord,"* not to mention being forever like Him, having received a glorified body in their resurrection just like He did in His.

Every born again child of God who is alive when Christ returns—unlike those who die before His return—will never find themselves in a bodiless state, or *"be found naked"* as Paul puts it in *2 Corinthians 5:3*. Rather, they shall *"be changed, in a moment, in the twinkling of an eye"* when their corruptible body *"puts on incorruption"* and their mortal body *"puts on immortality,"* (*1 Corinthians 15:51-53*). Once their glorified body is instantaneously put on over their fallen body they *"shall be caught up together with"* the resurrected *"dead in Christ. . .to*

meet the Lord in the air: and so shall [they] *ever be with the Lord,"*
(1 Thessalonians 4:17).

In spite of the fact that Paul hoped to be alive when
Christ came, so that he would never be bodiless, he still pre-
ferred being in God's presence in a bodiless state to continuing to be absent from God's presence in his fallen body. Paul
understood that God never intended for us to live in mortal
or fallen bodies. God's intention was for us to live in immortal bodies. According to Paul, it was for this *"selfsame thing"*
that God made us, *(2 Corinthians 5:4-5).* Paul even says that it
is to this end that God gives *"unto us the earnest of the Spirit."*
God gives us His Spirit, resulting in the rebirth of our spirit,
as a deposit guaranteeing what is to come; namely, the redemption of our bodies.

In *Romans 8:23* the Apostle Paul writes, *"And not only they,*
but ourselves also, which have the firstfruits of the Spirit, even we
ourselves groan within ourselves, waiting for the adoption, to wit, the
redemption of our body." Notice how Paul calls the Holy Spirit
"the firstfruits." The firstfruits were the first produce from the
harvest. They guaranteed that the rest of the harvest was to
come. It is no coincidence that the
Holy Spirit came on the Day of Pentecost. Pentecost was the Jewish
Feast of Firstfruits. The Holy Spirit
came on Pentecost because He is
the firstfruits of our salvation guaranteeing us that the rest is to come.

> God gives us His
> Spirit, resulting in
> the rebirth of our
> spirit, as a deposit
> guaranteeing what
> is to come; namely,
> the redemption of
> our bodies.

God's redemption of our spirits
is His guarantee that someday He
will also redeem our bodies. When that day comes, you and

I will once again be like God made us to be. We will be like Adam before the Fall and like Christ following His resurrection. Not only will we be alive spiritually, but we will be spiritually alive in a glorified body.

Until that glorious day comes when we shall receive our glorified bodies, the Apostle Paul admonishes us to *"faint not,"* (2 Corinthians 4:16-18). According to Paul, *"though our outward man perish,"* we shouldn't be discouraged because our *"inward man is renewed day by day."* Everyday our fallen body is perishing or getting closer to falling off while our redeemed spirit is getting closer to breaking out and getting free from our fallen body. Far from being discouraged by this, we should be encouraged by it. After all, *"our light affliction, which is but for a moment, worketh for us a far more exceeding and eternal weight of glory."* Why should we be discouraged by the fleeting troubles we are currently experiencing in our temporal bodies when we have an immortal body waiting on us in eternal glory?

Along with showing us why we should not be discouraged, Paul also teaches us how to keep from it. He instructs us to *"look not at the things which are seen, but at the things which are unseen: for the things which are seen are temporal; but the things which are unseen are eternal."* You and I should not live by what we see, the corruptible, but by what we can't see, the incorruptible. In other words, we shouldn't live according to the flesh, but according to the Spirit.

In 2 Corinthians 5:7, the Apostle Paul teaches us to *"walk by faith, not by sight."* You and I must not live by *"sight."* We must not live by what our corruptible bodies see and gather from this corruptible world. Instead, we must live by *"faith."*

We must believe and obey all that God speaks to our spirit through His Spirit. Living by faith, or in the Spirit, instead of by sight, or in the flesh, will deliver us from discouragement!

> Why should we be discouraged by the fleeting troubles we are currently experiencing in our temporal bodies when we have an immortal body waiting on us in eternal glory?

The Bible teaches us that Christ has given His glory to every Christian, see *John 17:22* and *2 Thessalonians 2:14*. We have the glory of Christ within us. However, His glory is presently veiled by our flesh, just as it was by His during His earthly sojourn. Remember, Christ partook of our flesh so that He could die for our sins, *(Hebrews 2:14)*. He had to come into our world in a corruptible body in order to be able to die in our place. Without a corruptible body Christ would not have been subject to death.

According to *Philippians 2:5-8*, Christ possessed the fullness of His glory in the form of God before His incarnation. Nevertheless, in His incarnation the fullness of His glory was emptied into the form of a man. The Greek word *"kenoo,"* which Paul uses in *verse 7*, means to empty the contents of one vessel into another. This is why Paul says in *Colossians 2:9*, "*For in* [Christ] *dwelleth all the fullness of the Godhead bodily.*" All of God was emptied into a corruptible body in the man Christ Jesus. This is the miracle of the incarnation!

Since Christ's glory was emptied into a corruptible body in His incarnation it became veiled by His flesh. This explains how Isaiah could say of Christ: "*He hath no form nor comeliness; and when we shall see him, there is no beauty that we should desire him."* With His glory veiled by His flesh Christ appeared common or ordinary in His earthly appearance.

In *Mark 9:1-8*, we have Mark's account of the transfiguration of Christ. On the Mount of Transfiguration Christ pulled back the robe of His flesh revealing the glory within Him to Peter, James and John. Interestingly, the Greek word for *"transfigured"* is the word we get *"metamorphosis"* from. Metamorphosis is when the caterpillar emerges from the cocoon as a butterfly.

> All of God was emptied into a corruptible body in the man Christ Jesus. This is the miracle of the incarnation!

Before Jesus took Peter, James and John up on the Mount of Transfiguration He promised to some who were with Him that they would *"not taste of death, till they [saw] the kingdom of God come with power."* Christ was promising them that once He ascended to the throne and was given all power and authority He would come to rule and reign in their hearts in the power of the Holy Spirit. On the Day of Pentecost Christ's promise was fulfilled. The kingdom of God came into the hearts of believers with power.

Christ invades the lives of believers in all of His glory in the person of the Holy Spirit. It is the Holy Spirit that deposits Christ's glory in us. That glory, however, is presently veiled by our flesh. This is what Paul is talking about in *2 Corinthians 4:7-18*. Still, just as all of God was in Christ, but veiled by His flesh, all of Christ is in us, but veiled by our flesh, (*Colossians 2:9-10*).

In *Romans 8:17-25*, the Apostle Paul teaches us that all of creation is waiting in *"earnest expectation. . .for the manifestation of the sons of God."* All of creation is longing and waiting for the glory of Christ to be made manifest in the children of God by *"the redemption of our bodies."* When Christ returns and we receive our glorified bodies His glory in us will no longer be concealed by our flesh. Instead, it will be revealed by our glorified bodies, just as God's glory in Christ was no longer concealed, but revealed following Christ's resurrection. The fact that Christ's appearances were glorious ones following His resurrection explains why His disciples had such a hard time recognizing Him.

When Jesus returns to the earth in His glorified body His glory will be revealed to the whole world, *(Matthew 25:31-32)*. Also, you and I will receive our glorified bodies when Christ returns in His. As the Apostle John puts it, *"When [Christ] shall appear, we shall be like him; for we shall see him as he is,"* *(1 John 3:2)*. No longer will the glory of Christ be shrouded by our fallen bodies. Instead, thanks to our glorified bodies, Christ's glory in us will at long last be displayed by us. In addition to this, Paul teaches that when Christ returns *"creation itself also shall be delivered from the bondage of corruption into the glorious liberty of the children of God."* The whole earth will be delivered from corruption and filled with God's glory. All of creation, including you and I—God's new creation in Christ—will once again be doing what it was created to do; manifesting and displaying the glory of God. As the ancient

> Just as all of God was in Christ, but veiled by His flesh, all of Christ is in us, but veiled by our flesh.

> All of creation, including you and I — God's new creation in Christ — will once again be doing what it was created to do; manifesting and displaying the glory of God.

prophet Habakkuk predicted, *"For the earth shall be filled with the knowledge of the glory of the Lord, as the waters cover the sea,"* (Habakkuk 2:14). Is there any wonder then that the Apostle Paul wrote that *"the whole creation groaneth and travaileth in pain"* waiting with *"earnest expectation"* for the *"manifestation of the sons of God?"*

THE RENEWING OF MAN'S MIND

Christ's first coming resulted in the redemption of our spirits. His second coming will result in the redemption of our bodies. He came the first time for our spiritual resurrection. He is coming again for our physical resurrection. When He returns our spiritual life, which is presently *"hid with Christ in God,"* shall be revealed when you and I shall *"appear with him in glory,"* (*Colossians 3:1-4*). Until then, the Apostle Paul says that you and I are to *"seek"* and *"set our affections"* on *"those things which are above, where Christ sitteth on the right hand of God."* We are not to set our affections *"on things on the earth."*

As born again children of God you and I must live by what our King speaks from His throne to our hearts through the person of the Holy Spirit. We must no longer live, as we always have, by the faulty information of a fallen world received through the five senses of our fallen bodies and processed by the understanding of our fallen minds. To put it more succinctly: we must be reprogrammed. As Paul writes in *Romans 12:2*, *"And be not conformed to this world: but be ye transformed by the renewing of your mind, that ye may prove what is the good, and acceptable, and perfect, will of God."*

Why do most Christians today believe, even though the Scripture fails to support it, that they have two natures? And why are the vast majority of today's Christians defeated in their spiritual lives by what they mistakenly believe to be

their old sinful nature? I submit for your careful consideration that it is merely because they are deceived. They are receiving and believing the wrong readouts. They are still "*conformed to this world.*" They are still living the way the lost world does—in the flesh. They are living by what their fallen minds make out of the faulty information they receive from this fallen world through the five senses of their fallen bodies. They have never reprogrammed themselves, or renewed their minds. They have never started living in the Spirit. Although they have the capacity to do so, now that they are born again, they are still not living by what Christ speaks to their spirit through the person of the Holy Spirit who lives within them.

In all fairness to today's Christians, most of them have never been taught to renew their minds. Thus, even though they have come to Christ and been born again, receiving the capacity to live in the Spirit, they continue to live as they always have—in the flesh. It is, after all, the only way they know how to live. No one has ever bothered to teach them differently. Perhaps, one reason for this is that many of today's Christian teachers don't know any better themselves. If they did, they wouldn't be teaching us all that we have two natures.

In *Philippians 2:5* the Apostle Paul writes, *"Let this mind be in you, which was also in Christ Jesus."* As Christians you and I are to think the same way Christ did. How did Christ think? In *John 5:30* Jesus said, *"I can of mine own self do nothing: as I hear, I judge: and my judgment is just; because I seek not mine own will, but the will of the Father which sent me."* Notice, Jesus judged things according to what He heard. In other words, Jesus lived His earthly life by every word He heard the Father speaking to Him. He did not live His earthly life by the way everything in this fallen world appeared to Him through the five senses of His mortal body. In fact, He condemned the people of His day for judging by appearances, *(John 7:24)*.

Although Jesus was God, He did not live His life on this earth as God. Instead, He lived His life on this earth as a man. This explains how He could say, *"I can of mine own self do nothing."* Why would Christ limit Himself to living as a man during His earthly life? Let me assure you that the multiple answer to this question will provide you with some of the most important truths you'll ever learn.

> **Although Jesus was God, He did not live His life on this earth as God. Instead, He lived His life on this earth as a man.**

There are at least three reasons why Christ limited Himself to living as a man during His earthly sojourn. To begin with, Christ could not have died for the sins of all men had He not first lived a sinless life as a man. Only by living sinlessly as a man could Christ become man's sin substitute on the cross of Calvary, *(Hebrews 2:9-18)*. Secondly, Christ had to live as a man in order to be able to sympathize with us and intercede for us as our great High Priest, *(Hebrews 4:14-15; 7:25)*. Finally, and most importantly for our study, Christ had to limit Himself to living as a man during His earthly sojourn so that He could set the perfect example of how every man should live. This is why the Apostle John called Christ *"the true Light, which lighteth every man that cometh into the world," (John 1:9)*. Jesus Christ is *"the true Light"* who has brought to light the way God intends for *"every man that cometh into the world"* to live. The Apostle Peter echoed the Apostle John when he taught us to *"follow [Christ] steps,"* because He has left us a perfect *"example," (1 Peter 2:21)*.

How did Christ live? He lived His whole life in response to what the Father said. As we have already seen, He thought what the Father told Him to think, *(John 5:30)*. He also did what the Father told Him to do and said what the Father told Him to say, see *John 5:19; 12:49*. Truly, Christ lived His earthly life by every word that proceeded out of His Father's mouth.

How are you and I to live? We are to live as Christ did. Remember, He is our perfect example. You and I are to live our whole life in response to what Christ says. We are to think what He tells us to think. We are to do what He tells us to do. We are to say what He tells us to say. In short, we are to live our lives by every word Christ speaks to our hearts through the person of the Holy Spirit who lives within us.

When we do we will be living in the Spirit. As Jesus said in *John 6:63*, *"the words that I speak unto you, they are Spirit, and they are life."*

It is at this point that some will take exception to our teaching. They will insist that God doesn't speak to us directly today, but only indirectly. According to them, we speak to God through prayer and He speaks to us through the Bible, others and circumstances. If this is true, then what kind of a relationship can you and I ever hope for with God?

Let's suppose that the only way your spouse would ever communicate with you was indirectly. She would only communicate with you through a love letter she wrote to someone else a long time ago, through other people or third parties, and occasionally through circumstances; leaving you certain signs within them to figure out for yourself. What kind of marriage could you possibly hope for under these terms? Obviously, you would have no hope at all for a successful marriage. Likewise, you and I have no hope at all for a successful Christian life if these are the terms of our relationship with God.

> There is absolutely no way that you and I can follow the example Jesus left for us if God doesn't speak directly to us just as He did to Jesus.

There is absolutely no way that you and I can follow the example Jesus left for us if God doesn't speak directly to us just as He did to Jesus. How can we live as God intends us to and as Jesus did; *"by every word that proceedeth out of the mouth of God,"* if you and I can't hear God? Regardless of what some may think, God does speak directly to His children today just as He did to His Son long ago. God speaks directly to us today through the person of the Holy Spirit who lives within us.

In *John 16:5-7*, Jesus told His disciples that it was better for them that He was going away. How could this possibly be true? How could Jesus going away be the best thing for us? According to Jesus, His going away was best for us because it would result in Him sending *"the Comforter"* to us. Who is this Comforter that Jesus promised to send? The Comforter is none other than the Holy Spirit.

Why was it better for us that Jesus left and the Holy Spirit came? Until the ascension of our Lord and the arrival of the Holy Spirit, Jesus lived among us, but not within us. During His earthly life Jesus was living in our world. If you wanted to be with Him you had to be wherever He was. However, now that He has ascended and the Holy Spirit arrived Jesus lives in us. Therefore, we no longer have to be wherever He is, because He is always with us wherever we are! This is exactly what Jesus was talking about when He said, *"And I will pray the Father, and he shall give you another Comforter, that he may abide with you forever; Even the Spirit of truth; whom the world cannot receive, because it seeth him not, neither knoweth him: but ye know him: for he dwelleth with you, and shall be in you. I will not leave you comfortless: I will come to you. Yet a little while, and the world seeth me no more; but ye see me: because I live, ye shall live also. At that day ye shall know that I am in my Father, and ye in me, and I in you,"* (John 14:16-20).

Now that Jesus lives in us in the person of the Holy Spirit we have everything we need to live the Christian life. Everything we need is in our heart, since Christ now resides there in the person of the Holy Spirit. Although Christ is seated in

heaven at the right hand of the Father so that He can intercede for our lives, see *Romans 8:34,* He is also—thanks to the
indwelling Holy Spirit—seated on the throne of our hearts so
that He can intervene in our lives. Thus, the Apostle Paul
assures us that we have no need of *"ascending into heaven. . .to
bring Christ down,"* because Christ *"is nigh [us]. . .even in [our]
hearts,"* *(Romans 10:6-8).*

Since Christ lives in our hearts in the person of the Holy
Spirit you and I know all we need to know. Jesus promised
us that when the Holy Spirit came He would *"teach [us] all
things"* and *"guide [us] into all truth,"* *(John 14:26, 16:13).* The
Apostle John went so far as to say that we already *"know all
things,"* thanks to the *"unction"* we've received *"from the Holy
One,"* *(1 John 2:20).* Just think about it, you already have all
the answers since He who knows all things lives in your heart
in the person of the Holy Spirit.

In *1 John 2:27,* John teaches us that *"the anointing* [Holy
Spirit] *which we have received of him* [Christ] *abides in us, and we
need not that any man teach us: but as the same anointing teaches
us of all things, and is truth, and is no lie, and even as it hath
taught us, we should abide in him."* What other teacher do we
need than the Master Teacher Him-
self who *"abides in us"* in the person
of the Holy Spirit? Whatever He
teaches us we know we can *"abide
in,"* because His teaching is always
the *"truth"* and never a *"lie."* Unlike
the teaching of men, what Christ
teaches us is never mistaken nor

> You already have
> all the answers
> since He who
> knows all things
> lives in your heart
> in the person of
> the Holy Spirit.

misleading. Consequently, you and I can live confidently by

whatever Christ says to us through the person of the Holy Spirit who lives within us.

Along with exhorting us to think like Christ, the Apostle Paul also assures us that we are capable of doing so. In *1 Corinthians 2:16*, Paul teaches us that every Christian has *"the mind of Christ."* According to Paul, no one can know the thoughts of a man, but *"the spirit of man which is in him,"* (*1 Corinthians 2:11*). Likewise, no man can know the thoughts of God, *"but the Spirit of God."* Since we have received the Spirit of God you and I can know God's thoughts, (*1 Corinthians 2:12*). Thanks to the indwelling Holy Spirit we have the capacity to know what Christ thinks, or as Paul puts it: *"We have the mind of Christ."*

Having the mind of Christ does not necessarily mean that every Christian lives the way Christ thinks he should. The truth is, most Christians have never brought *"into captivity* [their] *every thought to the obedience of Christ,"* (*2 Corinthians 10:5*). Instead of living by what Christ thinks, which can only be revealed to us by the indwelling Holy Spirit, see *1 Corinthians 2:12-14*, the majority of today's Christians are still living by what they think. Having failed to renew or reprogram their minds they continue living in conformity to our fallen world and in consistency with the way they always have.

Tragically, when we fail to live in the Spirit, or by what Christ thinks, which is revealed to us by the indwelling Holy Spirit, and continue to live in the flesh, or by what our fallen minds think about the faulty information we receive from this fallen world through the five senses of our fallen bodies, we are doomed to live the rest of our lives by the wrong read-

outs. This inevitably leads to deception and defeat. The Bible
is rife with examples that prove this point. For instance, consider with me the tragic tale of Israel's wilderness wanderings.

After miraculously delivering Israel from their slavery in
Egypt and miraculously providing for them in the wilderness, God led Israel to the fords of the Jordan; the threshold
of Canaan. Canaan was called the Promised Land, because
God had promised it to Israel. According to the Apostle

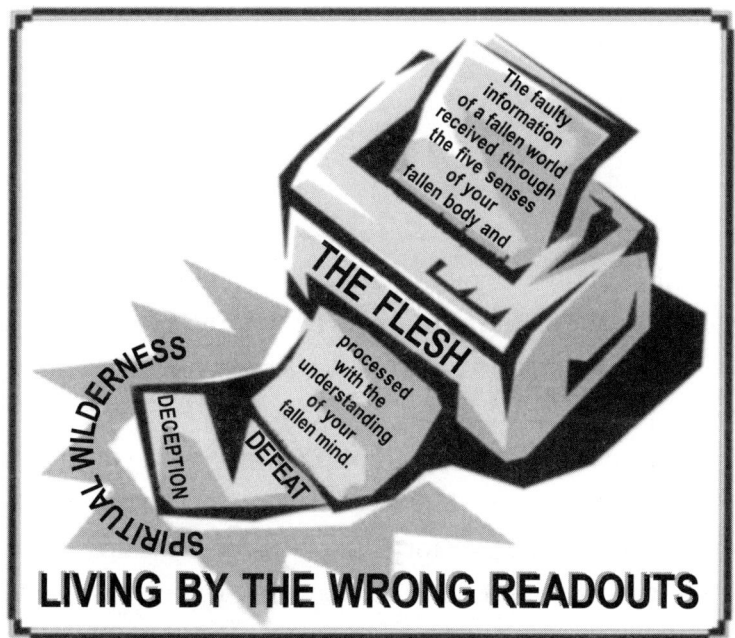

LIVING BY THE WRONG READOUTS

Paul, there are no ifs, ands or buts in the promises of God,
(2 Corinthians 1:19-20). Whatever God has promised we
can possess. Therefore, all Israel needed to do was go in
and take possession of the land that God had promised
them.

Before entering the land and taking possession of it,

Moses sent twelve Israelites to spy it out. Two of these spies, Joshua and Caleb, returned from the land and rehearsed for the people what God had said. According to them, the land was good just like God said it was. It was theirs, since God had promised it to them. And the time had come to go in and possess it. After all, wasn't that what God had commanded them to do? The other ten spies, unlike Joshua and Caleb, did not rehearse for the people what God had said. Instead, they reported to the people what they had seen. According to them, the land was filled with warring people, fortified cities and even giants. In view of this, they strongly advised against obeying God and entering the land. There was just simply no way that they could see for Israel to conquer the Canaanites and capture Canaan.

Unfortunately, Israel believed the evil report of the ten spies instead of the good report of the two. They subsequently refused to cross Jordan and enter into Canaan. As a result of their disbelief and disobedience God swore in His wrath that that whole generation, with the exception of Caleb and Joshua, would die in the wilderness and never enter into Canaan. For forty years that generation of unbelievers wandered around in circles in the wilderness. Finally, they all died in their unbelief without ever stepping foot into the land that God had promised them.

Contrary to popular opinion, Canaan does not represent heaven. Instead, Canaan is an Old Testament picture of the Spirit-filled victorious Christian life. Israel did not have to wait to the hereafter to enter Canaan, but was commanded by God to take possession of it in the here and now. Likewise, you and I are not to wait till we get to heaven to live in the Spirit, but are to do so here and now.

Like Israel, all we have to do to enter Canaan, or live in the Spirit, is believe and obey what God says. By living our lives according to all that Jesus is saying to us through the indwelling Holy Spirit, you and I can enter, experience and enjoy all that God has promised us in Christ. However, if we decide like Israel, in particularly like the ten spies, to live by what we see, instead of by what Christ says, we will spend the rest of our Christian lives going around in circles on a spiritual carousel.

Have you been wondering why you seem to be going around in circles in your spiritual life? No matter what you try you just can't seem to get anywhere. Although you believe and profess that all of God's promises are true, you can't honestly say that you are possessing them and experiencing them in your daily life. It is as though you are lost in some kind of spiritual wilderness. Well, now you know what your problem is. You are living in the flesh. You are living by what your fallen mind makes out of the faulty information you receive from this fallen world through the five senses of your fallen body. You are not living in the Spirit. You are not living by what Christ speaks to your heart through the person of the Holy Spirit who lives within you. If you continue living in the flesh, refusing to renew your mind so that you can live in

> By living our lives according to all that Jesus is saying to us through the indwelling Holy Spirit, you and I can enter, experience and enjoy all that God has promised us in Christ.

the Spirit, you are doomed to die in your spiritual wilderness. Like unbelieving Israel, you too will live out the rest of your life without ever stepping foot into all that God has promised you in Christ.

The author of the book of Hebrews boldly declared that *"There remaineth therefore a rest for the people of God," (Hebrews 4:9)*. Even today there is a Promised Land to be possessed by God's people. Today's Promised Land, however, is not a geographical place, but an abundant life that Jesus came to give us, *(John 10:10)*. Our Promised Land is possessed by our living in the Spirit. It does not require our relocating to a certain vicinity in the Middle East.

In view of the fact that there still remains a Promised Land to be possessed by the people of God today, the book of Hebrews issues to us this solemn warning: *"Wherefore (as the Holy Ghost saith, Today if ye will hear his voice, Harden not your hearts, as in the provocation, in the day of temptation in the wilderness: When your fathers tempted me, proved me, and saw my works forty years. Wherefore I was grieved with that generation, and said, They do always err in their heart; and they have not, known my ways. So I sware in my wrath, They shall not enter into my rest.) Take heed, brethren, lest there be in any of you an evil heart of unbelief, in departing from the living God. . .But with whom was he grieved forty years? was it not with them that had sinned, whose carcasses fell in the wilderness? And to whom sware he that they should not enter into his rest, but to them that believed not? So we see that they could not enter in because of unbelief. Let us therefore fear, lest, a promise being left us of entering into his rest, any of you should seem to come short of it," (Hebrews 3:7-12, 17-19; 4:1).*

Conclusion

If you walk into any Christian bookstore today you will find a number of books that teach you how to get along with your spouse, raise your kids, handle your finances, manage your time, share your faith, study your Bible, conduct your prayer life, grow your church; ad infinitum. Along with these voluminous volumes you will also find all of those confusing titles. One title suggest that there are 10 keys to living in the Spirit. Another implies that there are 5 secrets to living a successful Christian life. And a third boast that its pages contain the 12 steps to Christian victory. Well, which is it: ten keys, five secrets or twelve steps? Who knows?

In *2 Corinthians 11:3* the Apostle Paul expressed his fear that *"the serpent"* would beguile the Corinthian Christians and lead them away *"from the simplicity that is in Christ."* A visit to any of today's Christian bookstores should be enough to convince anyone that what Paul feared happening to the Corinthians has happened to us. *"The serpent"* has definitely slithered his way into today's church and led us away from simple lives of devotion to Christ. We have made the Christian life so complicated, not to mention so confusing, that today's Christians have practically no hope at all of ever living it.

Is the Christian life really all that complicated? Do you and I need to read all those books and acquire all that knowledge in order to do all those things in our Christian lives. And how about those ten keys, five secrets and twelve steps; which of them do we need to subscribe to? You'll probably

be relieved to learn that all you really need to live in the
Spirit can be found in one verse of Scripture.

In *John 2:1-11* we are told about our Lord's first miracle—
changing the water to wine. Mary; the mother of Jesus, Jesus'
disciples, and Jesus Himself had all been invited to a wedding in Cana of Galilee. During the wedding an embarrass-
ing situation arose. The wine reserves for the wedding feast
began to run low. Becoming aware of the impending embar-
rassment Mary reported the need to her Son.

Jesus' response to His mother: *"Woman what have I to do
with thee,"* has been misunderstood and misinterpreted by
many. Some have even suggested that Jesus was being disre-
spectful. Nothing could be further from the truth. All Christ
was doing was informing Mary that He did not take His or-
ders from her, but only from headquarters. He was not dic-
tated to by the tyranny of the urgent. He only did what His
Father told Him to do. When He checked in with His Father on this occasion He saw Him making wine. Therefore,
Christ joined His Father in it and made some Himself!

Mary's words in *John 2:5* to the servants at the wedding
in Cana, *"Whatsoever he saith unto you, do it,"* are her last re-
corded words in all of Scripture. They are also all of the
Scripture you will ever need to live the rest of your life in the
Spirit. Living in the Spirit is as simple as doing whatever
Christ tells you to do.

You will be living in the Spirit whenever you are doing
what Christ is telling you to do through the person of the
Holy Spirit who lives within you. You don't need 10 keys, 5
secrets, nor 12 steps. You just need to do *"whatsoever he saith
unto you."* Likewise, when you are doing whatever He is tell-

ing you to do you won't need to read all those books on how to get along with your spouse, raise your kids, handle your finances, manage your time, share your faith, study your Bible, conduct your prayer life and grow your church. All of these things will fall into place and take care of themselves.

Years ago I went to hear a preacher of some renown. When he arose to speak he informed us that his topic for the evening was "How To Live In The Spirit." He then proceeded to inform us that he had three points. By this time I was beginning to regret that I had wasted the time to drive such a considerable distance to hear this well-known speaker. The last thing I felt like I needed was another man-made formula for living in the Spirit. However, I was soon to find myself pleasantly surprised.

The first point of this popular preacher's sermon was to simply to do the next thing that the Holy Spirit tells you to do. His second point was identical to his first, "Do the next thing that the Holy Spirit tells you to do." His final point, as you may have guessed by now, was no different, "Do the next thing that the Holy Spirit tells you to do." To this day that sermon is still the best I've ever heard on how to live in the Spirit. In fact, I

> The simple truth is, all you need to do to live in the Spirit is the next thing that the Holy Spirit tells you to do!

don't believe it can be improved upon. The simple truth is, all you need to do to live in the Spirit is the next thing that the Holy Spirit tells you to do!

THE KING OF HEARTS

I had heard of His splendor
His glory was world renowned
So I searched diligently the heavens
For this King with the diadem crown

They say His power is earth-shaking
The most powerful of realms He disdains
For while all earthly kingdoms will tumble
His shall forever remain

Where is the throne room of the universe
Where I may find His Mercy Seat
And bow my way to forgiveness
As time and eternity meet

I searched the land of His earthly sojourn
In the city where Israel's great kings once reigned
I looked in the cathedrals of the world's great churches
Which were erected and stood for His name

Yet futile were all my efforts
So despairingly I gave up the quest
Then my eyes fell upon an elderly Christian
To whom I made one last desperate request

Sir, could you tell me the place of your king's palace
Where I may find Him seated to rule
For I have searched the whole world over
And am convinced the earth's not His throne, but a stool

In response to my heartfelt question
The old Christian pointed to his breast
And encouraged me to cease from my wanderings
And at last grant my soul its rest

He said the kingdom of God doesn't come with observation
That I would never find it in chapel, senate, or mart
For the kingdom of God was within men
And the King I sought was enthroned in his heart

NOTES

If you would like to order
additional copies of this book,
or if you would like to schedule
the author as a speaker, please
write us at:

PRESS WORTHY
P.O. BOX 5476
SPRING HILL, FL 34611

Press Worthy